THERE'S A TRICERATOPS IN THE TREE HOUSE

IN THE TREE HOUSE

Aleksei Bitskoff & Ruth Symons

QEB Publishing

Triceratops was a big, plant-eating dinosaur with three

Design: Duck Egg Blue
Managing Editor: Victoria Garrard
Design Manager: Anna Lubecka
Dinosaur Expert: Chris Jarvis

Copyright © QEB Publishing 2013

First published in the United States by
QEB Publishing, Inc.
3 Wrigley, Suite A
Irvine, CA 92618

www.qed-publishing.co.uk

All rights reserved. No part of this publication may be reproduced, stored in a retrieval system, or transmitted in any form or by any means, electronic, mechanical, photocopying, recording, or otherwise, without the prior permission of the publisher, nor be otherwise circulated in any form of binding or cover other than that in which it is published and without a similar condition being imposed on the subsequent purchaser.

A CIP record for this book is available from the Library of Congress.

ISBN 978 1 60992 533 8

Printed in China

massive horns on his head!

He lived around **70 million** years ago—several millions of years before the first humans appeared.

But just imagine if Triceratops was alive today! How would he cope with modern life?

What if Triceratops joined a soccer team?

He had sturdy legs for racing up and down the field.

But he might POP the ball with his sharp horns!

With his 3 foot- (1 meter-) long horn the size of a hockey stick, Triceratops would be great at ice hockey.

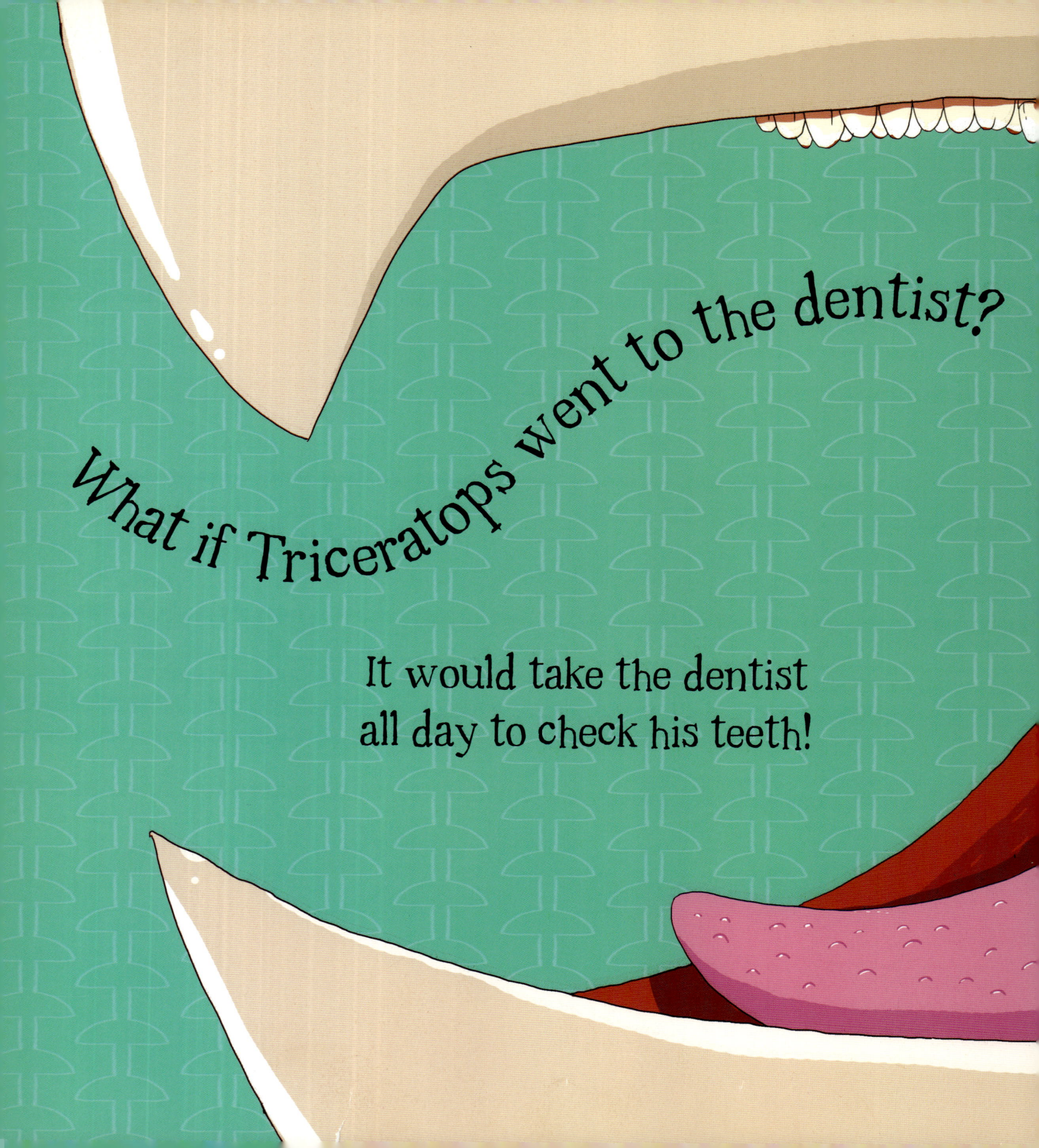

What if Triceratops went to the dentist?

It would take the dentist all day to check his teeth!

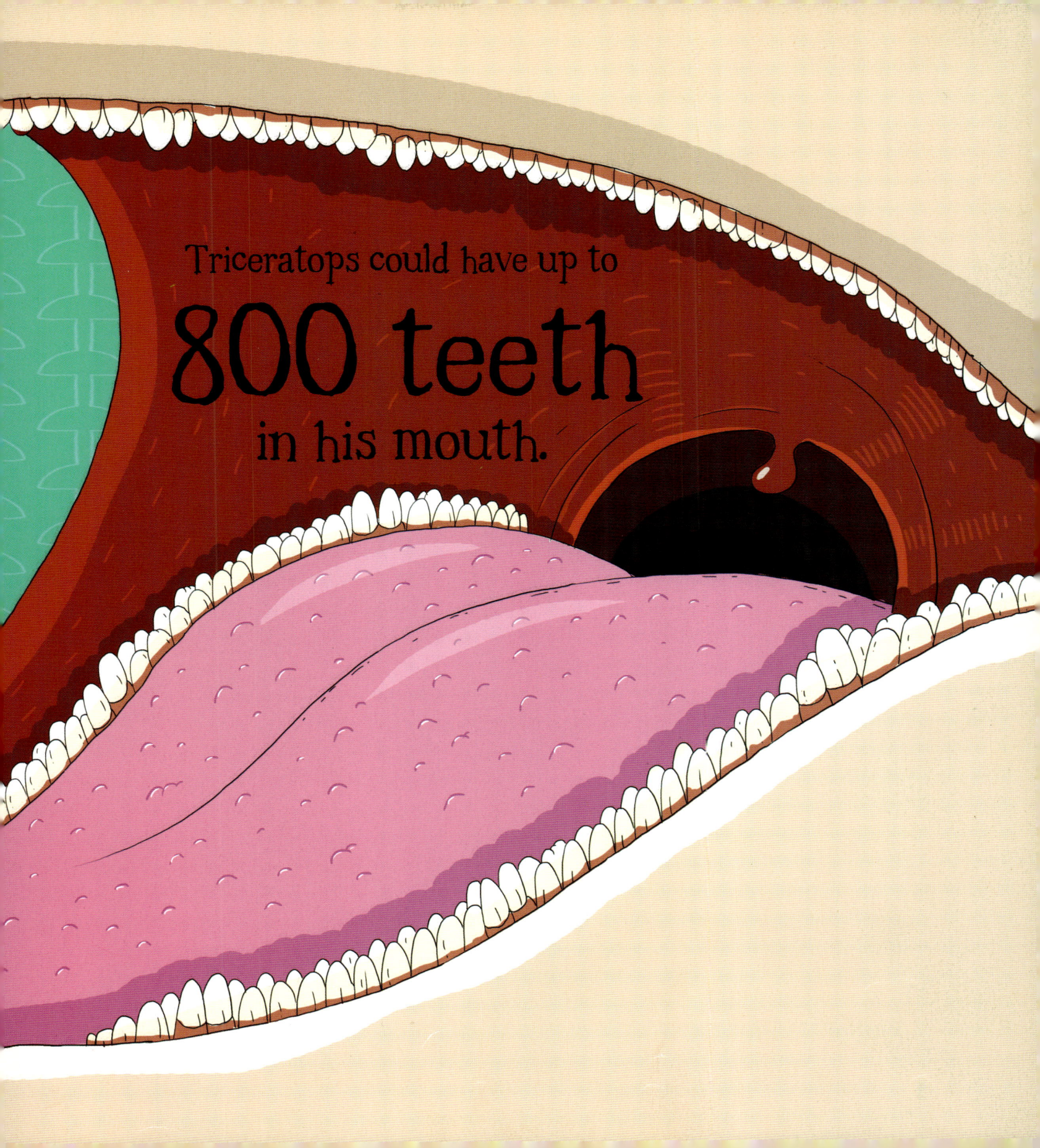

Triceratops could have up to

800 teeth

in his mouth.

What if Triceratops took the train?

At 30 feet (9 meters) long, Triceratops was almost the size of a train car.

He wouldn't fit in with the other passengers.

But he could travel in the **freight car!**

What if Triceratops went on vacation?

With his sharp, parrotlike beak, Triceratops could easily crack open coconuts. They would make a tasty drink for everyone on the beach!

But Triceratops would rather munch on palm leaves. His sharp teeth were perfect for slicing them up.

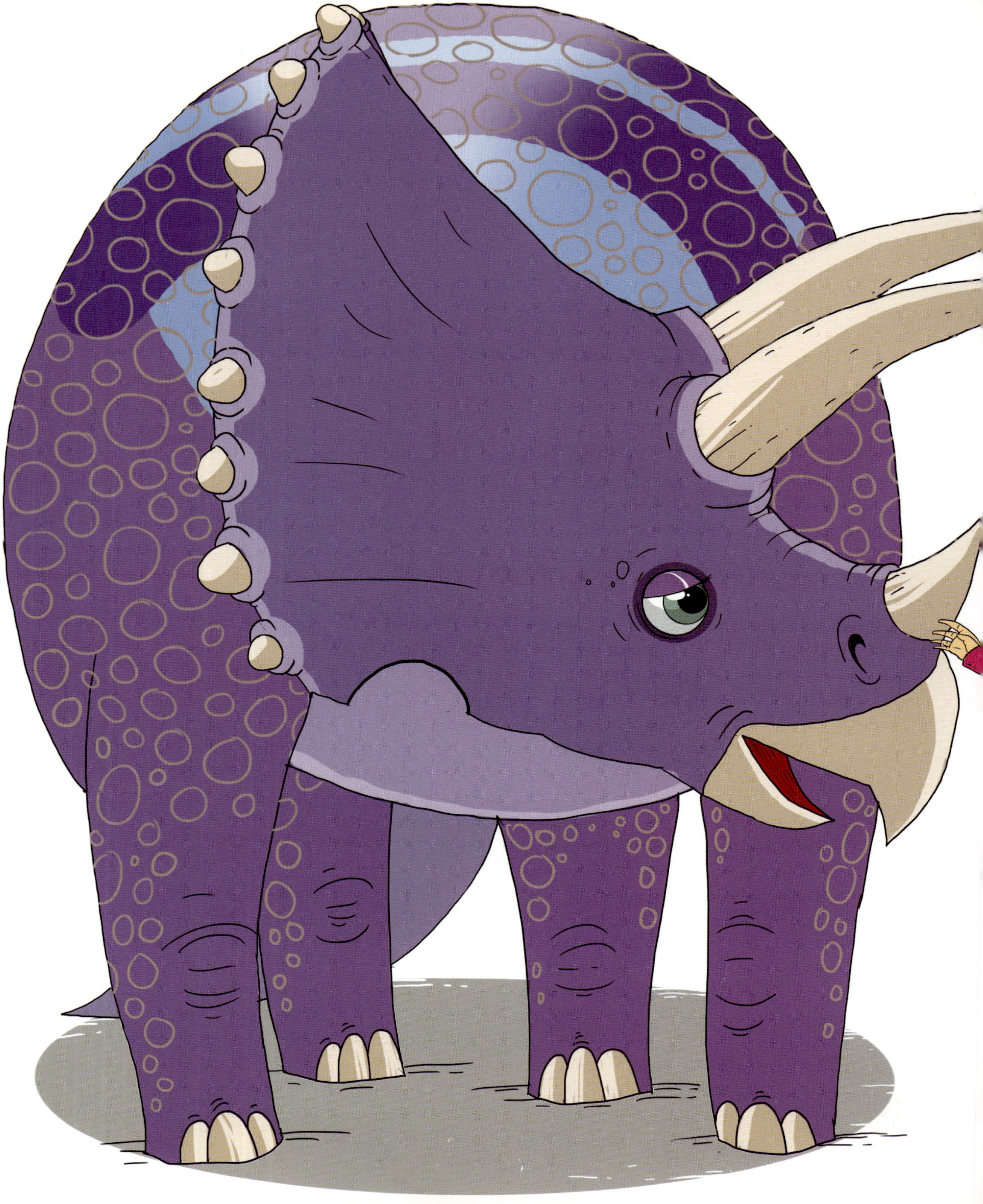

Was Triceratops taller than my dad?

Triceratops was much **taller** than any human. His skull alone was taller than your dad—it was 8 feet (2.5 meters) long!

A baby Triceratops was much smaller than its parents. Its head was only slightly bigger than yours!

What if Triceratops went on a school trip?

He would have a lot of fun—especially at a castle. He could pretend to fight like a knight!

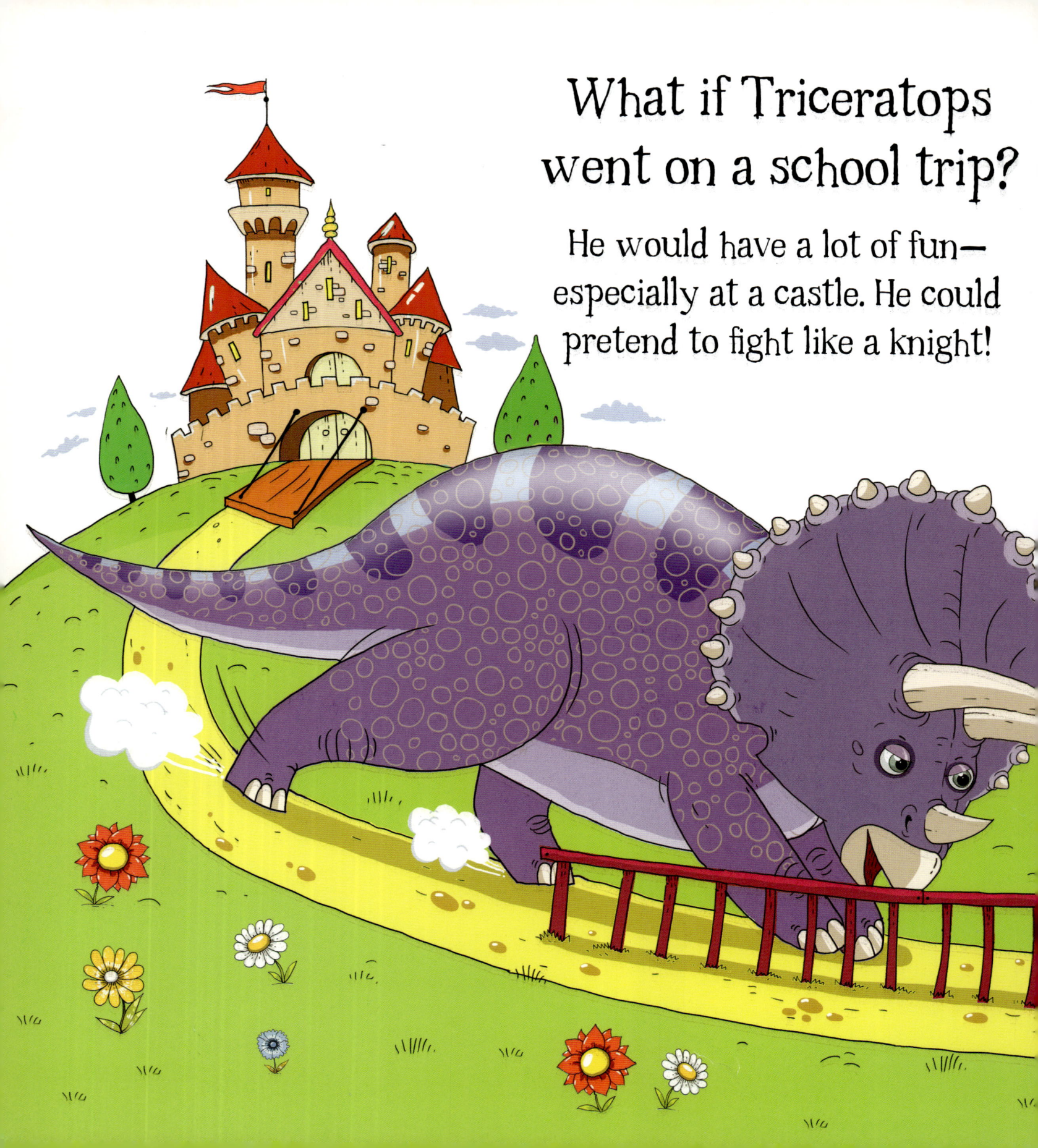

Triceratops wouldn't need armor because his thick skin was good protection.

He wouldn't need a lance because he had two long horns on his head.

And he was bigger than any horse!

What if Triceratops took a ride in a hot-air balloon?

It would have to be a very BIG balloon!

Triceratops weighed almost 5 tons (4.5 tonnes). That's as much as 200 children!

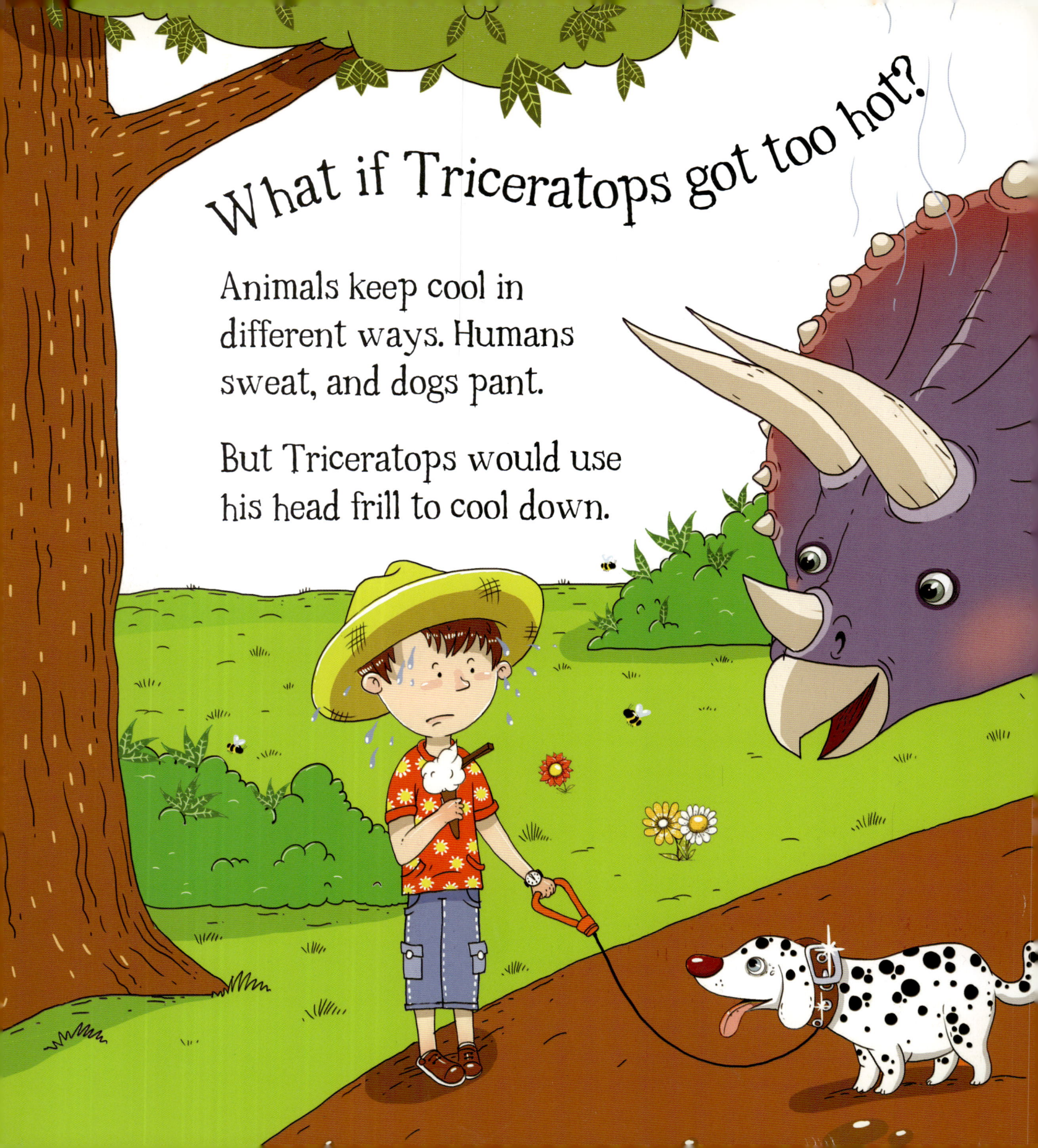

What if Triceratops got too hot?

Animals keep cool in different ways. Humans sweat, and dogs pant.

But Triceratops would use his head frill to cool down.

Blood flowing to the frill carried heat away from his body. He just had to find some shade or a nice cool breeze.

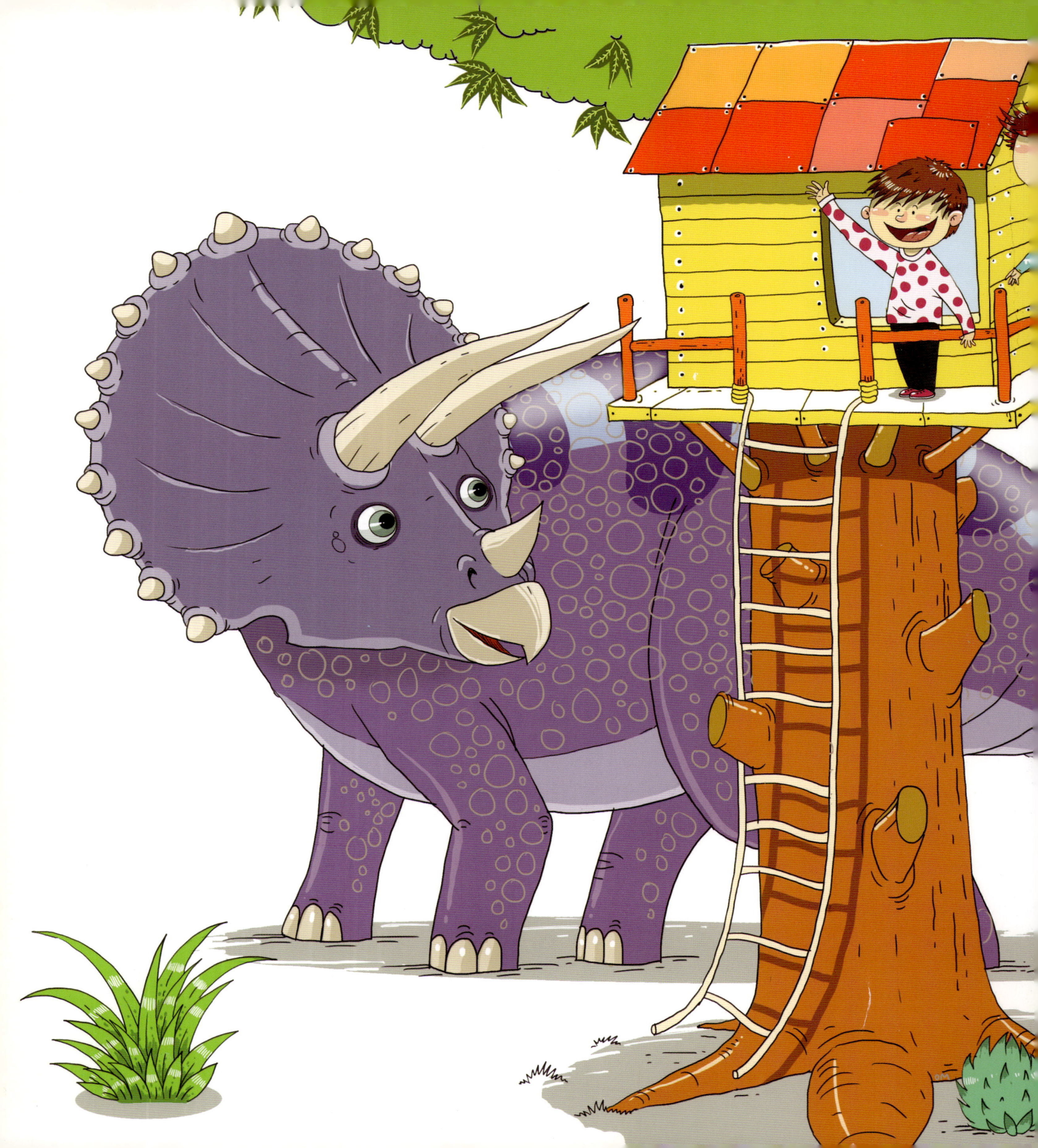

What if Triceratops came to my tree house?

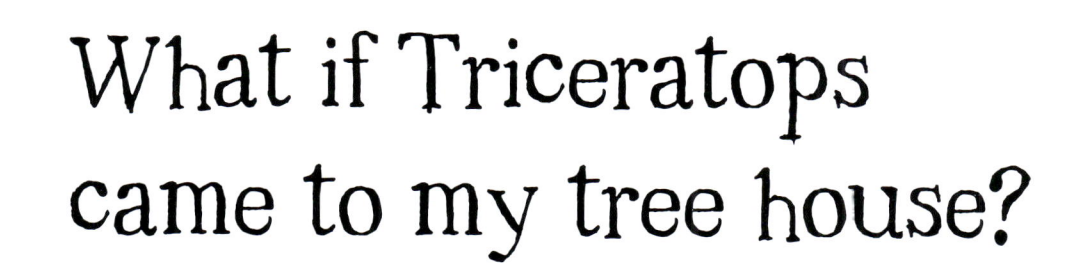

He'd be too **big** and **heavy** to get in the tree.

And his thick legs and chunky feet would make it hard to climb the ladder.

But he'd help you all get down!

Triceratops's skeleton

Everything we know about Triceratops comes from fossils—skeletons that have been in the ground for thousands and thousands of years.

Scientists can look at fossils to figure out how dinosaurs lived in the past.

This means that we know a lot about dinosaurs, even though no one has ever seen one!

X-RAY 1192289775982-69
MODEL No.: nx110005306 195714613344

big, heavy tail

thick, sturdy legs

DINO SCAN: TRICERATOPS BODY (SIDE)

- bulky body
- large head frill
- two long horns
- one short horn
- sharp beak

ALBERTA, CANADA
Complete skeleton discovered—2012

WYOMING, U.S.A.
Fossil skull found—1888

COLORADO, U.S.A.
First fossil horns discovered—1887

NEW YORK, U.S.A.
Biggest skull found—2012

MONTANA, U.S.A.
Fossil of baby Triceratops found—2006

PASSPORT

Triceratops
(TRY-SAIR-A-TOPS)

NAME MEANS "THREE-HORNED FACE"

WEIGHT 5 TONS (4.5 TONNES)

LENGTH 30 FEET (9 METERS)

HEIGHT 10 FEET (3 METERS)

HABITAT SCRUBLAND, BUSH, PRAIRIES

DIET FERNS, PALM LEAVES, OTHER PLANTS

T<TRI<<TRICERATOPS<<<<<<<<<<<632107254374523<<<<<<<<<<<<<0032622976542501>>>>>>>